MARTIAL ARTS IN ACTION

WRESTLING

MARTIAL ARTS IN ACTION

WRESTLING

BY CAROL ELLIS

mc **Marshall Cavendish**
Benchmark
New York

Published by Marshall Cavendish Benchmark
An imprint of Marshall Cavendish Corporation

Other Marshall Cavendish Offices:
Marshall Cavendish International (Asia) Private Limited, 1 New Industrial Road, Singapore
536196 • Marshall Cavendish International (Thailand) Co Ltd. 253 Asoke, 12th Flr, Sukhumvit
21 Road, Klongtoey Nua, Wattana, Bangkok 10110, Thailand • Marshall Cavendish (Malaysia)
Sdn Bhd, Times Subang, Lot 46, Subang Hi-Tech Industrial Park, Batu Tiga, 40000 Shah Alam,
Selangor Darul Ehsan, Malaysia

Marshall Cavendish is a trademark of Times Publishing Limited

All websites were available and accurate when this book was sent to press.

Library of Congress Cataloging-in-Publication Data
Ellis, Carol, 1945-
Wrestling / Carol Ellis.
p. cm. — (Martial arts in action)
Includes index.
ISBN 978-0-7614-4941-6
1. Wrestling—Juvenile literature. I. Title.
GV1195.3.E45 2011
796.812—dc22
2010013819

Editor: Karen Ang / Peter Mavrikis
Publisher: Michelle Bisson
Art Director: Anahid Hamparian
Series design by Kristen Branch
Photo research by Candlepants Incorporated
Cover Photo: William R. Sallaz / Getty Images

The photographs in this book are used by permission and through the courtesy of:
Getty Images: William R. Sallaz, 2, 26, 27, 42; Junko Kimura, 15; Paul Popper/Popperfoto, 17; 19;
Hulton Collection, 20; Ethan Miller, 22; Simon Bruty/Sports Illustrated, 24; Bob Martin/Sports Illustrated,
37, 38. *Corbis*: Dimitri lundt/TempSport, 6. *Super Stock*: Bridgeman Art Library, London, 8; Underwood
Photo Archive, 18; IndexStock, 30. *Alamy Images*: Dennis MacDonald, 9, 39; mikecranephotography.com,
16; Jim West, 21, 28, 32; Ilene MacDonald, 31; Image Source, 34; Visual&Written SL, 40. *Art Resource,
NY*: Erich Lessing, 10, 12; Réunion des Musées Nationaux, 14.

Printed in Malaysia (T)
1 3 5 6 4 2

CONTENTS

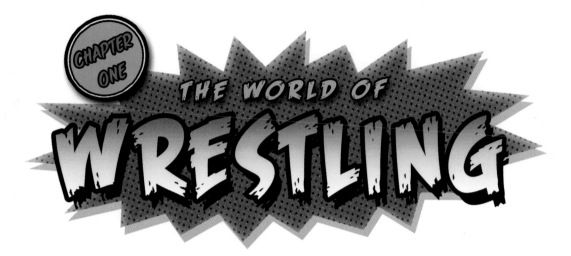

CHAPTER ONE

THE WORLD OF WRESTLING

THE YEAR IS 516 BCE. The place is Olympia, in ancient Greece. Two wrestlers face each other within a circle of sand. They have trained for weeks to get ready for the Olympic Games. Both of the competitors are from Croton, a Greek colony in what is now southern Italy. The younger athlete is Timasitheus. The people watching the wrestlers do not know much about Timasitheus, but they are familiar with his older opponent, Milo of Croton.

Milo of Croton is an unbeaten Olympic champion. He won the boys' wrestling crown more than twenty years ago, and has gone on to win many more competitions, including five Olympic crowns. Milo is a large man, and everyone has heard stories about how strong he is. No one is sure if the stories are true, but they are sure of one thing— young Timasitheus did not stand a chance against Milo of Croton.

WITH ITS ROOTS IN ANCIENT TIMES, MODERN WRESTLING IS A SPORT OF SKILL AND STRENGTH.

A FIFTEENTH-CENTURY SPANISH PAINTING CAPTURES TWO WRESTLERS IN MOTION.

TWO YOUNG WRESTLERS CIRCLE EACH OTHER, LOOKING TO MAKE THE RIGHT MOVE.

Timasitheus might not have been as strong as Milo, but he thought long and hard about how to beat Milo. Most wrestlers at that time used their strength to throw their opponents. Timasitheus decided to try a new **technique**. Instead of letting Milo get close enough to throw him, he would keep Milo at arm's length. If Timasitheus could stay out of Milo's powerful grasp, then he could probably gain the **advantage** and win.

Wrestling may seem like a simple test of pure strength, but it is also a game of strategy. To win, wrestlers need to use their minds as well as their muscles. Timasitheus had a carefully thought out **strategy**, and it worked. Milo of Croton could not grab Timasitheus, and was forced to chase him around. Milo grew too tired to keep fighting, and lost to Timasitheus.

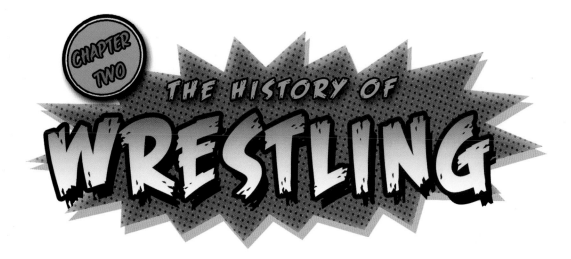

CHAPTER TWO

THE HISTORY OF WRESTLING

WRESTLING IS PROBABLY the oldest form of **unarmed combat** in the world. Early humans might have wrestled over supplies like food or places to live. They may have also used it to defend themselves from others. Around four thousand years ago in China, soldiers made wrestling a part of their military training. The samurai warriors of ancient Japan practiced sumo wrestling and developed jujitsu, a combination of wrestling, kicking, and striking, so they could keep fighting even if they lost their weapons. The **city-states** of ancient Greece were almost constantly at war, and when they were at peace, soldiers wrestled to keep fit and ready for the next battle.

Along with foot racing, wrestling is also one of the world's oldest sports. No one knows when the first wrestling match took place, but

CARVED IN MARBLE IN THE SIXTH CENTURY BCE, TWO GREEK WRESTLERS PIT THEIR SKILLS AGAINST ONE ANOTHER.

AN EGYPTIAN TOMB PAINTING SHOWS MEN USING WRESTLING TO TRAIN FOR COMBAT.

it grew from a form of combat into a popular sport in many ancient civilizations. Sumerians, who lived in what is now Iraq, wrestled for sport more than three thousand years ago. China and Japan both had forms of wrestling. Ancient Egyptian wrestlers used many of the same moves and **holds** that are seen in wrestling today.

ANCIENT GREECE AND ROME

Wrestling was especially popular in ancient Greece, where it was an important part of the culture. Most Greek cities had wrestling schools called **palaestras**. Along with reading, writing, and other

Wrestling in Ancient Art and Literature

- Scenes of people wrestling were painted on cave walls in France 15,000 to 20,000 years ago.

- The Sumerians, who lived in what is now Iraq, carved portraits of their wrestlers onto huge stone slabs at least five thousand years ago.

- In *Gilgamesh,* a Sumerian poem written around 2000 BCE, the king in the title is often called "Gilgamesh the wrestler" because of his wrestling skills.

- Hundreds of scenes of two men wrestling were engraved on the walls of ancient Egyptian tombs more than four thousand years ago. They show many of the same wrestling moves that are still practiced today.

- In the *Iliad,* which is about the battle for Troy, the ancient Greek poet Homer described a fierce wrestling match between the warriors Ajax and Odysseus.

ANCIENT GREEK ARTISTS OFTEN DEPICTED WRESTLING SCENES ON POTTERY.

subjects, schoolboys were expected to learn how to wrestle. The Greeks also turned sporting competition into an organized event. The Olympics, an athletic festival to honor the Greek gods, began in 776 BCE. The first recorded Olympic wrestling match took place in 708 BCE. When the athletes wrestled, they were covered in oil and coated in sand or dust so that they could get a better grip on each other.

There were two styles of wrestling. In upright wrestling, a contestant had to throw his opponent three times to win a match. In ground wrestling, the match went on until one of the contestants gave up. Biting and eye-gouging were against the rules. There was also a combination of wrestling and boxing, called **Pankration**. Pankration means "total victory," and it was brutal. Everything but eye-gouging and biting was allowed, even strangling. A match ended only when one of the contestants surrendered, lost consciousness, or died.

When the Roman Empire spread into Greece, the Romans included wrestling in their own games. Late in the fourth century CE, Roman emperors banned the Olympics. However, wrestling as a popular sport kept growing throughout the world.

JAPANESE CHILDREN LEARN THE SUMO RING-ENTRY CEREMONY. SUMO WRESTLERS USUALLY JOIN A STABLE WHEN THEY ARE TEENAGERS.

SUMO WRESTLING

Sumo wrestling is often called the national sport of Japan. According to legend, a wrestling match took place between two gods more than two thousand years ago, and the winner gained control of the Japanese islands. In ancient times, sumo was probably practiced at shrines and holy places to pray for a good rice harvest. The first recorded sumo match took place in 23 BCE. The victor was a potter named Sukune, who is known as the "Father of Sumo."

Today, sumo is a professional sport. The top-ranked wrestlers receive salaries. Both beginners and champions belong to stables, or schools, that are usually run by a retired wrestler.

Today's sumo wrestling still honors its ancient rituals. Before a fight, the wrestlers will clap their hands, calling the gods to watch over the match. They stamp their feet to crush any evil spirits, and

A SUMO RING IS 15 FEET (4.5 METERS) IN DIA-
METER AND IS COVERED WITH A THIN LAYER OF
SAND THAT ALLOWS THE WRESTLERS' FEET TO SLIDE.

toss salt into the ring to purify it. The actual match between the two
wrestlers does not usually last long. Some sumo matches can be over
in less than two minutes.

There are two ways to win: force your opponent out of the ring,
or make any part of his body except the soles of his feet touch the
ground. Sumo wrestlers often try to grab an opponent's belt to use
in a lift or throw. Sumo wrestlers are strong and weigh a lot so that
opponents have a harder time throwing or pushing them. Some sumo
wrestlers can weigh more than 300 pounds (136 kilograms)! Though
most sumo wrestlers are from Japan, many successful wrestlers come
from other Asian countries and even the United States.

WRESTLING IN EUROPE AND NORTH AMERICA

Backhold wrestling is an early martial art of Scotland that goes back as far as the seventh century CE. In today's form of backhold wrestling, opponents grip each other around the waist. A wrestler has his right hand under his opponent's left arm and his chin on the opponent's right shoulder. The first wrestler to make the other touch the ground or break the hold scores a point. The first one to get three points is the winner.

Glima began during the age of the Vikings. It has been practiced in Iceland for about one thousand years. Glima is a "trouser grip" style of wrestling. At the start of a match, the contestants grip each other's belts or the sides of their pants and try to throw each other to the ground.

GLIMA WRESTLERS GRAB HOLD OF LEATHER HARNESSES THAT ARE WORN AROUND THE WAIST AND THIGHS.

During the Middle Ages, kings and knights of Europe took part in wrestling matches. In 1520, King Henry VIII of England challenged King Francis I of France to a match. According to the story, King Francis won.

In Turkey, the oil wrestling championships have taken place every year since the 1600s. As many as one thousand wrestlers wearing oiled leather pants compete on a grassy field. Oil wrestling is an "anything-goes" style, and almost no holds or moves are forbidden.

In the early nineteenth century, the French developed a style of wrestling that did not allow any holds below the waist. This style came to be known as **Greco-Roman wrestling**.

Long before the Europeans settled in the American colonies, even before explorers set foot in North America, American Indians had their own forms of wrestling. When European settlers arrived, they brought their own styles from England, Scotland, and Ireland. One of the styles was called collar-and-elbow wrestling. Its name came from the way the wrestlers

TWO MEN BEGIN A MATCH USING THE COLLAR-AND-ELBOW STYLE OF WRESTLING.

FAMOUS WRESTLERS

Alexander Karelin of Russia has been called the greatest Greco-Roman wrestler of all time. Competing in the super-heavyweight class, he won gold medals in twelve European Championships, nine World Championships, and three Olympics. He was famous—and feared—for his reverse body lift, in which he lifted an opponent from the mat like a sack of potatoes and flung him feet-first over his head.

SUPER-HEAVYWEIGHT AND FOUR-TIME OLYMPIC CHAMPION BRUCE BAUMGARTNER WAS INDUCTED INTO THE U.S. OLYMPIC HALL OF FAME IN 2008.

Bruce Baumgartner of the United States was one of the most successful international freestyle wrestlers. He finished college with a record of 134 wins and only twelve losses. He was a four-time World Champion and won four Olympic medals—two golds, one silver, and one bronze. In the 1984 Olympics, Baumgartner became the first American in sixty years to win a gold medal in the super-heavyweight class.

AS WRESTLING GREW MORE POPULAR, THE CROWDS GREW LARGER.

started a match. They stood face to face, each gripping the other behind the neck and the elbow. George Washington, the first United States president, was a skilled collar-and-elbow wrestler.

The other style was called catch-as-catch-can wrestling, in which contestants could grab almost any part of an opponent's body. Before he became president, Abraham Lincoln made a name for himself in this rough style of wrestling. One of his most famous matches was with a man named Jack Armstrong. According to one person who watched the match, when Armstrong tried some moves that were not allowed, Lincoln "grabbed him by the neck and shook him like a toy." After that match, the two men became good friends.

As the United States grew, wrestling's popularity grew with it. The most popular style in America was called freestyle wrestling. It was developed from the rougher catch-as-catch-can style, and allows holds below the waist and on the legs.

WRESTLING COMPETITIONS

In 1896, the first Olympic Games of the modern age took place in Athens, Greece. Greco-Roman wrestling was one of the competitions. Freestyle wrestling became an Olympic sport in 1904.

WRESTLING IS NO LONGER A MEN-ONLY SPORT. THESE WOMEN FREESTYLE WRESTLERS ARE TRAINING FOR THE OLYMPICS.

PROFESSIONAL WRESTLING

Wrestling for prize money was popular in both Europe and the United States. It was a rough sport, but early professional wrestlers trained hard and fought to win. Over time, some forms of wrestling became more of a **spectacle** than a sport.

In today's professional wrestling, most of the wrestlers know how to fight, but they follow a script, or a plan. Some wrestlers are considered "good" or "bad" guys and the results of their fights are already planned out. Professional wrestling became even more popular when professional wrestling matches were shown on television. Today, professional wrestling is a very profitable form of entertainment.

PROFESSIONAL WRESTLING HAS ITS ORIGINS IN NINETEENTH-CENTURY CARNIVAL SIDESHOWS, WHERE CONTESTANTS SHOWED OFF THEIR STRENGTH AND ATHLETICISM.

Today, **amateur wrestling** can be seen in the Olympics, the World Championships, and the Pan American Games. Many high schools and colleges include wrestling in their athletic programs. Though it started out as a man's sport, wrestling is no longer just for men. Women's freestyle wrestling became part of the Olympic Games in 2004.

Today's amateur wrestling has rules, guidelines, and **weight classes** that ancient wrestlers did not use. But even with the changes, wrestling remains what it always was—two people using their minds and bodies to win a match.

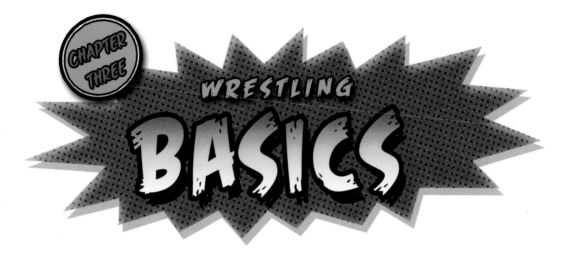

CHAPTER THREE

WRESTLING BASICS

TODAY, THERE ARE THREE BASIC STYLES of amateur competitive wrestling: freestyle, Greco-Roman, and folkstyle. Freestyle and Greco-Roman are the two styles used in international competitions, such as the Olympics and the Pan American Games. Folkstyle is also called collegiate wrestling. It is the style practiced in high schools, colleges, and clubs in the United States. It is very similar to freestyle. The main differences are in scoring and strategy.

In freestyle and folkstyle, wrestlers can use their arms, legs, and body to hold their opponents above and below the waist. Greco-Roman wrestlers use only their arms and upper bodies. They are not allowed to grab their opponents' legs or use any holds below the waist.

WOMEN WRESTLERS COMPETE IN A FREESTYLE MATCH.

WRESTLING MATCHES

No matter what the style, the goal of wrestling is the same. A wrestler must hold his or her opponent's shoulders to the mat for a certain number of seconds. This is called a **pin** or fall. Once this happens, the match is over. Wrestlers also earn points for successful moves and holds, such as forcing an opponent onto the mat, or recovering from a hold. If no pin occurs before the match's time limit is up, the wrestler with the most points gets the win. Wrestlers can also win before a match is over if they take the lead by a certain number of points.

A REFEREE MUST KNOW ALL THE RULES, MOVES, AND HOLDS IN ORDER TO MAKE THE RIGHT CALLS.

AT LARGE WRESTLING MEETS, MULTIPLE MATCHES OCCUR AT THE SAME TIME.

A wrestling match starts with two wrestlers facing each other on a large padded mat. The mat has two circles on it. The small circle in the center is where the match begins. The larger circle is the wrestling area. Wrestlers have to stay within the larger circle during the match.

Wrestlers begin a match standing in what is called the neutral position. Neither one has the advantage yet. A **referee** starts the match by blowing a whistle, and the wrestlers begin. The referee watches closely and awards points for different moves and holds. He also takes points away for **illegal** moves such as tripping an opponent or gripping his or her throat.

In the past, wrestling matches could last for hours. Today, there

LIKE ALL ATHLETES, WRESTLERS STRETCH THEIR MUSCLES TO AVOID INJURIES DURING A MATCH.

are time limits. International matches are six minutes long. If neither wrestler has scored any points, there may be three minutes of **overtime**. College matches are seven minutes long, and high school matches last for six minutes. A wrestling match is divided into three periods. In college, the first period is three minutes long and the second and third periods are two minutes each. In high school, the periods are each two minutes long.

Ancient wrestlers often faced opponents who outweighed them by many pounds. To keep a match fair and competitive, today's wrestlers are divided into weight classes that range from light-flyweight to super-heavyweight. In competitions, wrestlers are weighed before a match to make sure they are in the correct weight class. Because wrestlers rely on their bodies, they work hard to stay in shape. Stretching exercises loosen the muscles and help prevent injuries. Warm-ups like running or jumping rope get the blood flowing. Wrestlers in high school and college often lift weights to strengthen their muscles. But just like the young Greek wrestler, Timasitheus, who defeated wrestling champion Milo of Croton, today's wrestlers rely on strength and strategy. A wrestler learns hundreds of different moves and holds. Knowing when to use them is as important as being strong.

WRESTLING MOVES AND HOLDS

There are many different techniques in wrestling. The techniques are made of basic moves that a wrestler must practice. Putting these moves together in the right way helps a wrestler win a match without getting hurt or seriously hurting his or her opponent.

TWO YOUNG WRESTLERS ENGAGE IN A TIE-UP.

- **Body Throw**—A move in which the arms are locked around an opponent's body. The opponent is then thrown to the mat.
- **Breakdown**—To flatten an opponent so that he or she is on his or her stomach or side.
- **Escape**—To break free from an opponent's control.
- **Fireman's Carry**—A takedown move in which the opponent is temporarily brought over a wrestler's shoulders and then to the mat.
- **Grand Amplitude**—A throw in which an opponent is lifted

completely off of the mat and then brought down onto his or her back.

- **Half-Nelson**—A hold in which a wrestler's arm is under an opponent's armpit, with the wrestler's hand on the back of the opponent's head.
- **Lift**—To lift an opponent from the mat.
- **Reversal**—A move in which a wrestler is underneath an opponent or within a hold, but manages to regain control so that the opponent is on the bottom.

A WRESTLER TRIES TO AVOID A BREAKDOWN.

WRESTLING GEAR

You do not need much equipment to wrestle. When you first start, you can wear gym clothes and sneakers. Later, there are a few things you will need.

- **Singlet**—This one-piece nylon uniform fits closely and lets a wrestler move freely. In competition, wrestlers' singlets are usually in the color of their school or organization.

- **Shoes**—Wrestlers wear lightweight shoes that come up to the ankle. They have rubber soles and no heels, which give a wrestler support and flexibility.

- **Headgear**—Many wrestlers injure their ears during matches. For protection, wrestlers must wear headgear or ear guards. They have ear cups and are held in place by a buckle-free strap.

- **Knee Pads**—Wrestlers are not required to wear knee pads, but they can protect against bruising.

EAR GUARDS PROTECT WRESTLERS FROM "CAULIFLOWER EAR," AN INJURY CAUSED BY FRICTION AND REPEATED BANGING ON THE MAT.

- **Takedown**—To bring your opponent to the mat and gain control.
- **Throw**—Any move in which an opponent is lifted from the mat, then brought back down.
- **Tie-Up**—Any move in which a wrestler grabs an opponent's upper body to gain control.

WRESTLING IS PART OF THE athletic program in many high schools and colleges in the United States. Some middle schools also offer the sport. If your school does not have a wrestling program, or if you are younger than fourteen, there are clubs and camps where you can safely learn the sport. You should never try to learn wrestling moves on your own. When wrestling moves are done improperly, the fighters can be seriously injured.

Internet searches can help you find clubs and camps in your area. USA Wrestling, the organization that governs amateur wrestling in the United States, has information about different clubs and camps. Some gyms, athletic clubs, or martial arts studios also have wrestling classes.

FOCUS AND CONCENTRATION AS WELL AS STRENGTH ARE KEYS TO SUCCESS IN WRESTLING.

An Olympic Match

Rulon Gardner grew up on a dairy farm in Wyoming. He was big and chubby and was often teased about his size. Gardner worked hard on the farm, milking cows and carrying hay. By the time he was in high school, he could easily carry two 100-pound (45 kg) bales of hay under each arm. He started wrestling when he was in elementary school, and continued practicing through high school. Gardner had so much trouble with reading that some people thought he should forget about college. But with his parents' help, Gardner was able to attend a community college on a wrestling scholarship. Another wrestling scholarship sent him to the University of Nebraska, where he graduated with a teaching degree in physical education.

In 2000, Gardner stood in the center of the wrestling mat at the Olympics in Sydney, Australia. Facing him was the super-heavyweight champion, Alexander Karelin. Karelin grew up in Siberia. He often trained by running through thigh-deep snow for hours at a time. Karelin had not lost a match in thirteen years. This was his try at a fourth Olympic gold medal in Greco-Roman wrestling.

No one expected Rulon Gardner to win the match, but he did. He was so excited that he did a cartwheel after winning. Even though he is very proud of his Olympic win, Gardner said that the thing he was proudest of was getting a college degree—and wrestling helped him do it.

RULON GARDNER'S (RIGHT) WIN OVER ALEXANDER KARELIN (LEFT) WAS DUBBED THE "MIRACLE ON THE MAT."

A WRESTLER ATTEMPTS TO LIFT HIS OPPONENT OFF THE MAT.

Before signing up for wrestling, you should do careful research. Find out if the program or club has a good history of teaching students your age. Sit in on a class to see what the teachers and students are like. The most important thing is that you are comfortable and learning in a safe environment.

THE BENEFITS OF WRESTLING

Not everyone who wrestles ends up with a scholarship or Olympic medals. However, many people who are involved in the sport believe that there is more to wrestling than competitions. Wrestlers can gain

A YOUNG WRESTLER TRIES TO RECOVER FROM A HOLD.

A WRESTLER COMES CLOSE TO PINNING HIS OPPONENT.

more from the sport than learning how to perform a takedown or a body throw.

CONFIDENCE AND GOOD SELF-ESTEEM

Accomplishing goals helps build **confidence** and self-esteem. A person who accomplishes goals in wrestling, for example, often feels good about himself or herself. Wrestling is an individual sport.

A wrestler may belong to a team, but in a match, he or she has to rely on his or her own skills. Being a good wrestler is a personal achievement that a wrestler can feel good about. These good feelings can help the person feel better about accomplishing other goals. For example, some students say that the confidence they get from participating in matches in front of crowds helps them when they have to do presentations or other school activities in front of others. People with confidence and good self-esteem are usually happier or more satisfied with their lives.

FOCUS AND CONCENTRATION

There are many different moves that a wrestler must learn. This means that he or she must concentrate on what the teacher or coach is saying. Perfecting the moves requires a lot of practice. Wrestlers have to pay attention and concentrate on their opponents during matches or they can find themselves pinned. Some wrestlers say that the concentration they learn from wrestling helps them focus better in school.

PHYSICAL FITNESS

Experts and doctors say that everyone needs some form of physical activity to stay healthy and fit. Physical exercise helps maintain a healthy weight. It can also help with circulation, the immune system, and good mental health.

Wrestlers often work out and do stretching exercises to build muscles and stay flexible. When a person wrestles, all of the muscle groups in the body are being used. Exercising so many muscles can

EVENLY MATCHED IN SIZE AND WEIGHT,
TWO WRESTLERS STRUGGLE TO ACHIEVE
THE ADVANTAGE.

help a person stay in all-around good shape. Many high school athletes who play different sports wrestle during the **off-season** to stay fit. The skills learned in wrestling can improve strength, balance, coordination, and timing in other sports.

Almost anyone can learn how to wrestle. It is not a sport just for boys. You do not have to be the biggest, the strongest, or tallest athlete, because your opponent will always be about the same size as you. One of the world's oldest sports is a great way to have fun, to exercise, and to use both your muscles and your mind.

GLOSSARY

advantage—A favorable position.

amateur wrestling—Wrestling that is not a vocation for the competitors, as in Olympic, college, or high school wrestling.

city-state—An independent state consisting of a city and its surrounding territory.

confidence—A feeling of certainty.

Greco-Roman wrestling—A style of wrestling developed in the nineteenth century. A sporting event in the first modern Olympic Games.

holds—In wrestling and other martial arts, a method of grasping or clutching one's opponent.

illegal—In wrestling, this describes certain moves or positions that are against the rules.

off-season—The time of the year when there is no competition.

overtime—The time that goes beyond the set limit of a match. Most sporting events go into overtime if the score is tied.

palaestra—A wrestling school in ancient Greece.

Pankration—A combat sport dating back to the ancient Olympics that combines wrestling and boxing.

pin—In wrestling, to hold an opponent's shoulder to the mat for a few seconds. A pin is sometimes called a fall.

referee—An official who oversees a match and makes sure that the rules of the game are followed.

singlet—A tight-fitting, one-piece uniform used in amateur wrestling.

spectacle—An event or sport viewed as being entertaining.

strategy—A plan of action for accomplishing a goal.

technique—A special skill or set of movements.

unarmed combat—Fighting that is done without weapons.

weight classes—Levels of fighting determined by weight. Wrestlers in a weight class will compete against people who weigh about the same amount.

FIND OUT MORE

BOOKS

Chiu, David. *Wrestling: Rules, Tips, Strategy, and Safety.* New York: Rosen, 2005.

Linde, Barbara M. *Olympic Wrestling.* New York: Rosen, 2007.

Nardo, Don. *Wrestling.* San Diego: Lucent, 2002.

WEBSITES

FILA (International Association of Amateur Wrestling Styles)
http://www.fila-wrestling.com/index.php

National Wrestling Hall of Fame
http://www.wrestlinghalloffame.org/index.php

Sumo Wrestling—Kids Web Japan
http://web-japan.org/kidsweb/virtual/sumo/index.html

TheMat.com: (The Official Site of USA Wrestling)
http://www.themat.com/section.php?section_id=16

ABOUT THE AUTHOR

Carol Ellis has written several books for young people, including fictional mysteries and non-fiction books about pets and endangered animals. Her favorite sport is baseball, and while she has never taken up wrestling, she wrestled for fun with her older brother when she was growing up. She and her family share their New York home with two cats.